Creative Ways to Grieve

A Guided Grief Journal

Y. Y. Chan

This journal belongs to:

_____

In memory of:

_____

ISBN: 978-988-75589-1-0

Hong Kong

Chan, Y. Y.
Creative Ways to Grieve: A Guided Grief Journal /Y. Y. Chan

https://www.yychani.com

Little White Flowers
Publishing

Creative Ways to Grieve

Contents

And even if you lose yourself

And don't know what to do

The memory of love will see you through.

"Perhaps Love" by John Denver

Foreword

In 1981, John Denver wrote a song called **"Perhaps Love"** and asked Placido Domingo to sing it together. Whenever I think about all the people I've lost, I come back to the lyrics of this emotional song.

And even if you lose yourself
And don't know what to do
The memory of love will see you through

The memory of love never goes away and it can help you heal. When you are hurting the most, sit down and go back to happy times. Relive those memories and you will feel better, smiling at those precious keepsakes your loved ones have left behind. Your grief represents a treasure in itself, a teacher like no other. The lesson to be learned? Live today, live to the fullest!

Y. Y. Chan has created this beautiful grief journal to guide you through the healing journey. Journaling will help you deal with complicated emotions, but also to remember your loved ones and the wonderful moments spent together. As I see it, this grief journal will help you keep the memory of those you lost alive. With kindness and empathy, the author reminds you of all the things that mattered, so you can feel at peace with yourself.

Thanks to her selfless guidance, you might find the courage to do things that would have been otherwise difficult to try. For instance, writing a letter to someone you lost, expressing your emotions grief has brought to the surface, or taking some quiet time to reflect on your healing journey. The beautiful quotes sprinkled in-between will help you see grief as the "price of love", and not something to be denied.

I highly recommend this grief journal to anyone who is dealing with loss, finding it hard to heal. I have used it myself, and it was such a liberating experience, exactly the emotional release I needed.

I wish you a peaceful, healing journey!

Alexandra Antipa
Author – **Stories for the Heart: When Memories Become a Treasure** (grief memoir)
https://mybook.to/StoriesfortheHeart

From the Author

You never expect to lose someone you love. It can be painful and heartbreaking, and it can stay with you for the rest of your life. You never fully recover from loss and grief. You don't forget about it. You don't stop thinking about it. You don't stop missing and loving them – and you don't want to stop.

In the first couple of years after I lost my dad to pancreatic cancer, I didn't know what to do with all my emotions and feelings. Crying helped for a while but there seemed to be no end to the tears, and no real benefit to my healing. I started writing and journaling instead and tried writing a memoir about my experience. It was hard to recall a lot of the events and experiences and I wish I had recorded them down during that time. However, instead of giving up, I turned the memoir into a fictional children's book called *Can You Hear Me, Daddy?* Writing the story was such a therapeutic experience, which allowed me to express my emotions in a healthy manner. I wrote conversations I wish I could've had with my dad. Writing was my outlet and a form of communication with him after his death. I've never stopped talking to him since. It allowed me to use my creativity as well, imagining what we would talk about and what we could do together – even things we would never do in real life.

I had always dreamed about becoming an author and publishing my own book, but it wasn't until I experienced this great loss and grief that it unlocked something inside of me. I finally realized that my grief was a gift and I was able to use it to create something special and meaningful. Now whenever the tears come, they are no longer just full of pain or regret, but I also feel a sense of joy and hope, and think of creative ways I can express myself.

Grief is different for everyone, and you may experience a lot of mixed emotions. Don't suppress any of them when they come. Let them out and embrace them. Use them to create something special and long-lasting. This is why I created this journal. The world needs our stories and our masterpieces. Think about how many lives you can affect and impact with your creative work. It can be in all forms, such as paintings, movies, songs, poems, photography, etc. The possibilities are endless! The ideas and prompts in this journal will help get you started and help you unlock your creativity. Grief can lead to some of the most beautiful and impactful masterpieces in the world. It may feel like your loss is unbearable and your life will never be the same again, but I encourage you to explore your creativity and uncover your hidden talents with the help of this journal. Share your unique experience and new perspective with the world, or keep it for yourself to treasure the memories. Either way, your grief can become a gift and your superpower!

Join our Facebook community to share your story and masterpieces; connect with others and support each other. https://www.facebook.com/groups/creativityandgrief/

Y.Y.

How to Use this Journal

It can be daunting to start putting your thoughts and feelings down on a blank piece of paper without any guidance or prompts. Flip through the pages of this journal to find something that sparks a thought, an idea or a memory. Bookmark the pages you are interested in filling in. Select one a day or one every couple of days. Set your own schedule and timeline to complete it. You can complete them in any order you like, skip any you don't like or repeat ones you have enjoyed doing.

Make use of the Mood Tracker chart and Self-Care Tips at the beginning. Draw your emotion in the squares of the Mood Tracker chart for each day of the month. There are three pages for three months. Even if you do not complete any of the prompts, you can still chart your moods and observe any changes and patterns over the next few months. Set some simple goals on the bottom of the page, or simply select a few items from the Self-Care Tips to do.

There is also a section for Free Journaling without prompts, as well as blank pages for drawing, scrapbooking or note-taking. If you have your own ideas and find inspiration from other things around you, make use of them.

Though a lot of the pages in this journal provide lines for writing, you do not have to write. You can make a recording of your thoughts, film a video clip, sing a song, or even paint a picture in response. Do not feel constrained by the layout of this journal. Buy a blank journal or sketchbook and fill those pages up instead if you'd like. You can use this journal by yourself or together with your family. Make it a family project and create some masterpieces together. The most important thing is to find peace in something you enjoy doing. If you find it overwhelming or it makes you feel stressed, take a break. Don't force yourself to complete something if you don't enjoy it.

Share your creations and masterpieces with your friends and family and use them as an opportunity to start conversations about grief. Encourage one another to share openly about how they are feeling.

I hope this journal helps and inspires you to openly, freely and creatively express yourself, discover hidden gifts and talents within you, and make the grief journey a little easier.

Self-Care Tips

- Go for a walk or lie in the sun.
- Unplug and turn off your devices and spend time meditating or sitting in silence.
- If you are worried about something, set a specific time of the day to worry. Set a timer for 20 minutes. Write down all your worries and why they are bothering you. When the time is up, read aloud all the worries you have written down. You can turn it into a prayer.
- Similarly, set a time to cry. Let your tears out and allow yourself to be sad when you need to. Do not suppress your emotions.
- Do something you're good at. Continue to use your skills and abilities.
- Relax with a warm bath or wrap up in a blanket.
- Play some relaxing music or music that matches your mood.
- Write down what you did at the end of the day and how you felt.
- Find something to care for other than yourself or your family, such as a garden, a pet, or volunteer at an animal shelter.
- Breathe! Take deep breaths in through the nose and slowly out through the mouth. Practice mindfulness and pay attention to how your body moves and feels as you breathe.
- Say "No" to something… and "Yes" to yourself.
- Try gentle exercises like yoga, tai chi, or walking.
- Spend time in nature. Sit on the grass. Have a picnic. Go on a hike.
- Share your feelings with others you trust.
- It's OK to ask for and accept help. Your friends and family may want to support you but may not know what you need.
- Avoid isolation. Reach out to others and invite them over for a visit or go out together.

Mood Tracker

GOALS

NOTES

Mood Tracker

MONTH _____ 😃 🙂 😐 🙁 😢 😠 😴

GOALS

NOTES

_____
_____
_____
_____
_____
_____
_____
_____
_____
_____
_____

Mood Tracker

MONTH _____

GOALS

NOTES

_____

_____

_____

_____

_____

_____

_____

_____

_____

What we once enjoyed and deeply loved we can never lose, for all that we love deeply becomes part of us.

– Helen Keller

An Introduction

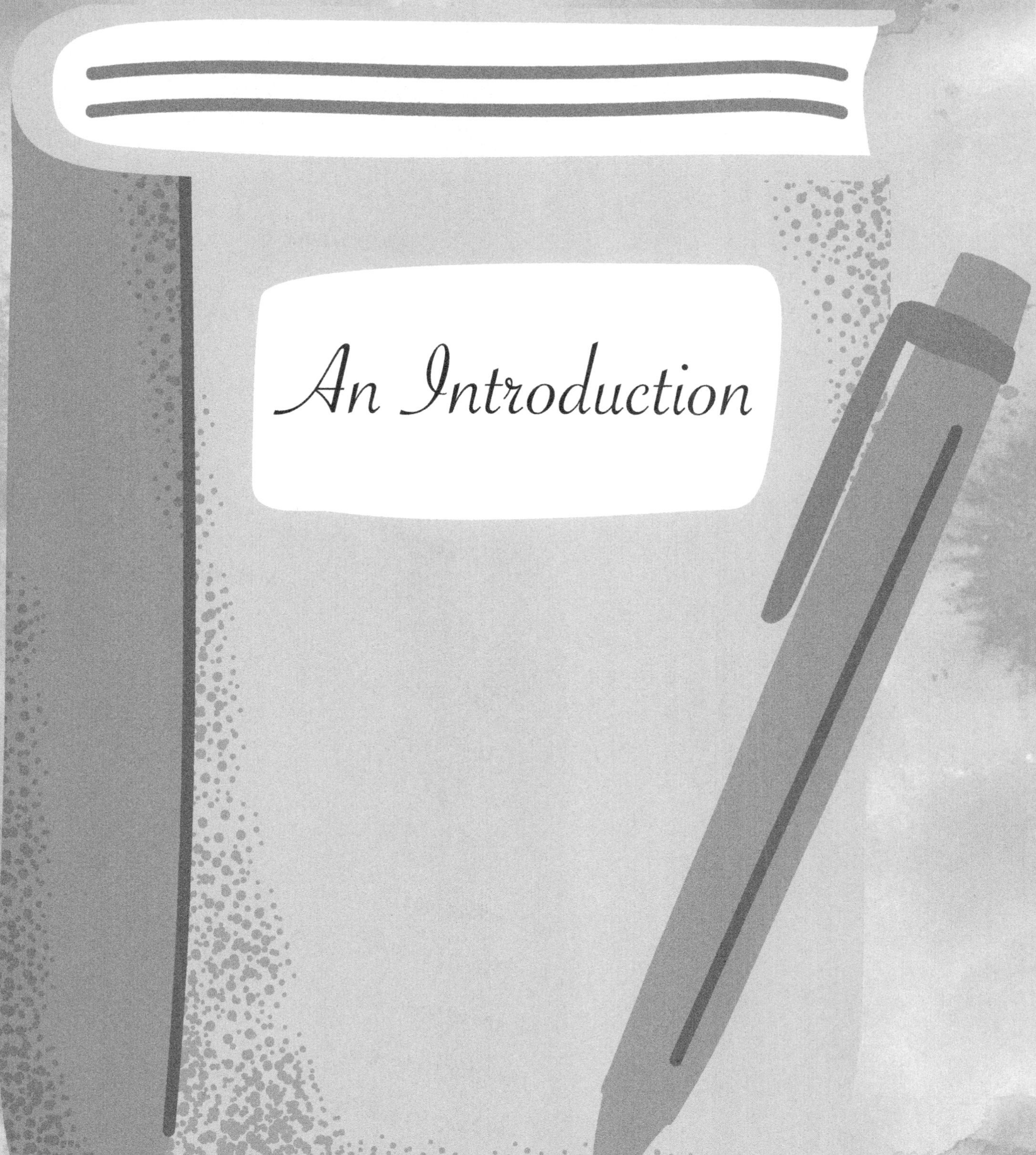

All About Me

Draw a picture here.

Add your photo here.

My name is:

My nickname is:

The people in my family are:

I live in:

What I like to do:

What I wish for:

My favorite food is:

My favorite sport is:

My favorite movie is:

My favorite book is:

My favorite place is:

All About My Family

Add your photo here.

Share something about each of your family members and what you love about them:

Draw a picture here.

What is the happiest or most memorable experience with your family?

Write a prayer or healing thoughts for your family:

What family traditions do you have?

All About My Loved One

PICTURE OF MY LOVED ONE

NAME / RELATIONSHIP

WHAT I LOVE ABOUT THEM

WHAT THEY LIKED / ENJOYED THE MOST

QUESTIONS I WANT TO ASK THEM

WHAT THEY DIDN'T LIKE

WHAT I ENJOYED DOING WITH MY LOVED ONE

All About My Loved One

WHAT I MISS MOST ABOUT THEM

SOMETHING THAT REMINDS ME OF THEM

MY FAVORITE MEMORY

A FUNNY THING THAT HAPPENED

WHAT I AM PROUD OF THEM FOR

THE LAST THING I TOLD THEM WAS...

The pain passes, but the beauty remains.

—Renoir

Daily Gratitude

Daily Gratitude

WHAT I AM THANKFUL FOR TODAY

It's important to reflect on your day and think about all the good and positive things that happened. Even if it feels like nothing 'good' or significant happened, try to think about the bright side. Stuck in traffic? Maybe it gave you time to listen to an audiobook or your favorite songs; or you were able to pause, look out the window and enjoy the scenery. Your dinner plans got canceled? Maybe it gave you the chance to spend quiet time reading or go somewhere you haven't been before. You can even be grateful for what *didn't* happen. Try seeing things from a different perspective. Write a few sentences about what you are thankful for each day, even if it's something small.

Date: _____

_____

_____

_____

_____

_____

_____

Daily Gratitude

WHAT I AM THANKFUL FOR TODAY

Date: _____

_____

_____

_____

_____

_____

Date: _____

_____

_____

_____

_____

_____

Daily Gratitude

WHAT I AM THANKFUL FOR TODAY

Date: _____

_____

_____

_____

_____

_____

Date: _____

_____

_____

_____

_____

_____

Daily Gratitude

WHAT I AM THANKFUL FOR TODAY

Date: _____

_____

_____

_____

_____

_____

Date: _____

_____

_____

_____

_____

_____

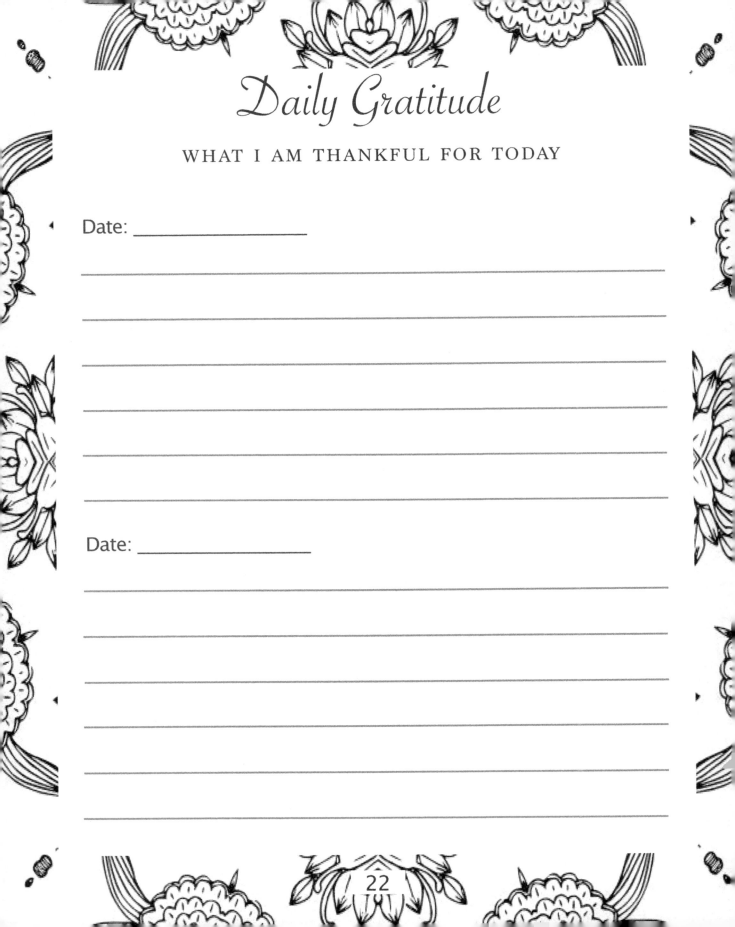

Daily Gratitude

WHAT I AM THANKFUL FOR TODAY

Date: _____

_____

_____

_____

_____

_____

Date: _____

_____

_____

_____

_____

_____

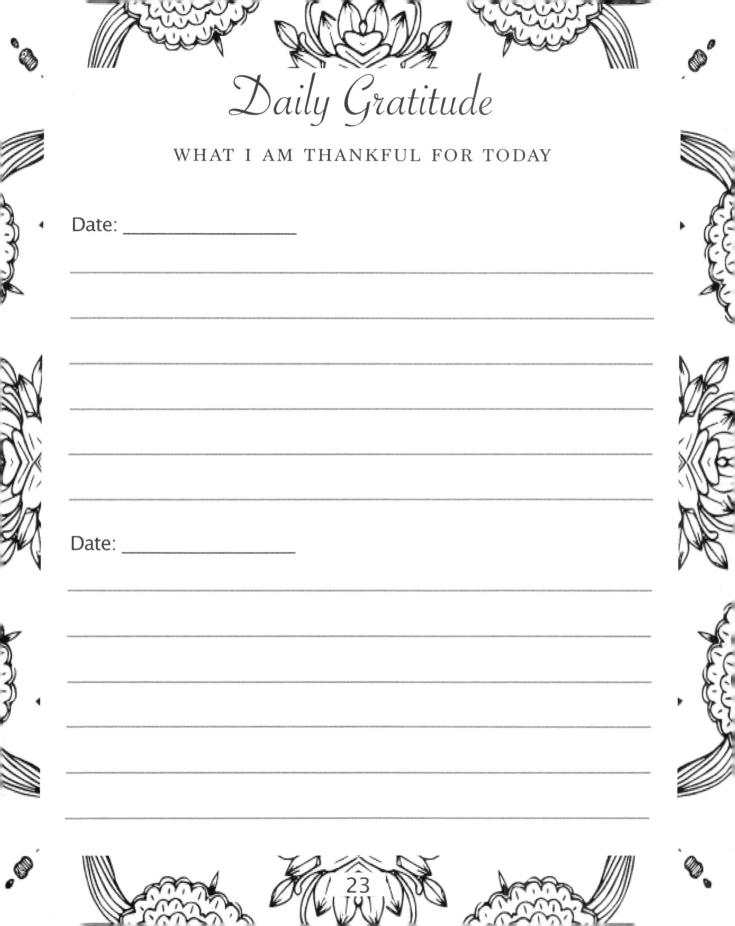

Daily Gratitude

WHAT I AM THANKFUL FOR TODAY

Date: _____

_____

_____

_____

_____

_____

_____

Date: _____

_____

_____

_____

_____

_____

_____

Daily Gratitude

WHAT I AM THANKFUL FOR TODAY

Date: _____

_____

_____

_____

_____

_____

Date: _____

_____

_____

_____

_____

_____

Gratitude Jar

Continue to practice daily gratitude with a Gratitude Jar.

1. Get a jar.
2. Decorate the jar (paint, add stickers, etc.).
3. Cut up strips of paper and put them by the jar.
4. Write down something you are grateful for each morning or evening on a strip of paper (add the date if you'd like). It can be something very simple, something that made you smile, laugh, or helped you in some way. (See some examples below.)
5. Put it inside the jar. (You can write more than one a day.)
6. Take them out at the end of the month and read through them.
7. You may want to keep them as reminders and encouragement for when you are feeling sad or down.
8. If this exercise has helped you, keep going, start a new jar.

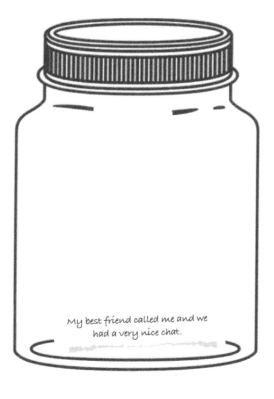

I saw a beautiful rainbow when I woke up this morning.

I was able to spend some quiet time alone and read my favorite book.

My best friend called me and we had a very nice chat.

Your life was a blessing, your memory a treasure. You are loved beyond words, and missed beyond measure.

–Unknown

Precious Memories

Precious Memories

MY FAVORITE MEMORY OF YOU

What is your favorite memory of your loved one and why is it so special?

Date: _____

_____

_____

_____

_____

_____

_____

_____

_____

_____

_____

_____

_____

Precious Memories

WHAT I ADMIRE ABOUT YOU

Write three to five things that you admire about your loved one.

Date: _____

_____

_____

_____

_____

_____

_____

_____

_____

_____

_____

_____

_____

Precious Memories

RELIVE A DAY

If you could relive a day in the past with your loved one, which one would it be? Describe the day and what made it so special.

Date: _____

_____

_____

_____

_____

_____

_____

_____

_____

_____

_____

_____

Precious Memories

THINGS THAT REMIND ME OF YOU

Write about the things that remind you of them, and why.
What moment or memory does it remind you of?

Date: _____

_____

_____

_____

_____

_____

_____

_____

_____

_____

_____

_____

Precious Memories

THE FUNNIEST MEMORY

Write about a funny moment or memory you have of your loved one.
Why was it so funny? How do you feel when you think about it now?

Date: _____

_____

_____

_____

_____

_____

_____

_____

_____

_____

_____

_____

_____

Memory Box

Make a memory box and fill it with your loved one's favorite things or items that remind you of them. List some of them on this page or draw a picture of them.

You can use an old shoe box and decorate the box with pictures of your loved one.

You can also decorate the box using rice paper decoupage. Use the whole sheet or tear the rice paper into small pieces and stick them onto the box.

Here's a video tutorial you can watch:

https://www.youtube.com/watch?v=F5Tg3Ax6QRw

At the blueness of the skies and in the warmth of summer, we remember them.

— Sylvan Kamens & Rabbi Jack Reimer

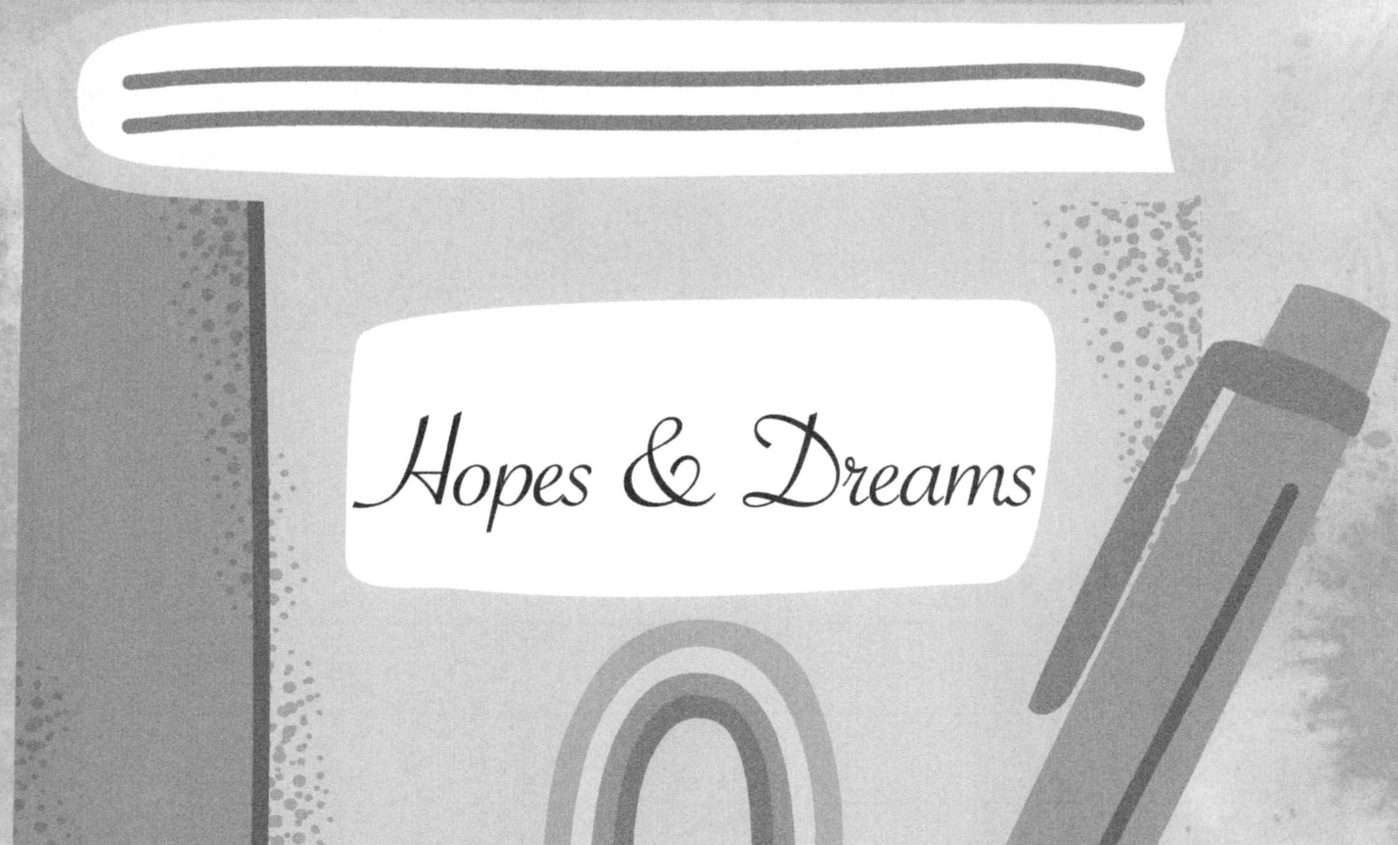
Hopes & Dreams

Hopes & Dreams
WHAT I WISH I COULD DO WITH YOU

Write what you wish you could do with your loved one, and why.

Date: _____

_____

_____

_____

_____

_____

_____

_____

_____

_____

_____

_____

Hopes & Dreams

I WISH I COULD TELL YOU . . .

Write about something you wish you could tell your loved one. Maybe it's a secret, something you're proud of, something you wish they knew, etc.

Date: _____

_____

_____

_____

_____

_____

_____

_____

_____

_____

_____

_____

Hopes & Dreams

MY GOALS FOR MY HEALTH

Write down some goals you want to set for your health – physically and mentally. What will you do more of? What will you do less of?

Date: _____

_____

_____

_____

_____

_____

_____

_____

_____

_____

_____

_____

Hopes & Dreams

MY GOALS FOR MY FUTURE

Write down some goals you want to set for your future. Where do you see yourself in five to ten years? What do you want to achieve?

Date: _____

_____

_____

_____

_____

_____

_____

_____

_____

_____

_____

_____

Hopes & Dreams

I HAD A DREAM ABOUT YOU

Write about a dream you had of your loved one. Where were you? What were you doing? How did you feel?

Date: _____

_____

_____

_____

_____

_____

_____

_____

_____

_____

_____

_____

_____

_____

Date: _____

Give the sorrow words; the grief that does not speak knits up the o-er wrought heart and bids it break.

–William Shakespeare

Letters

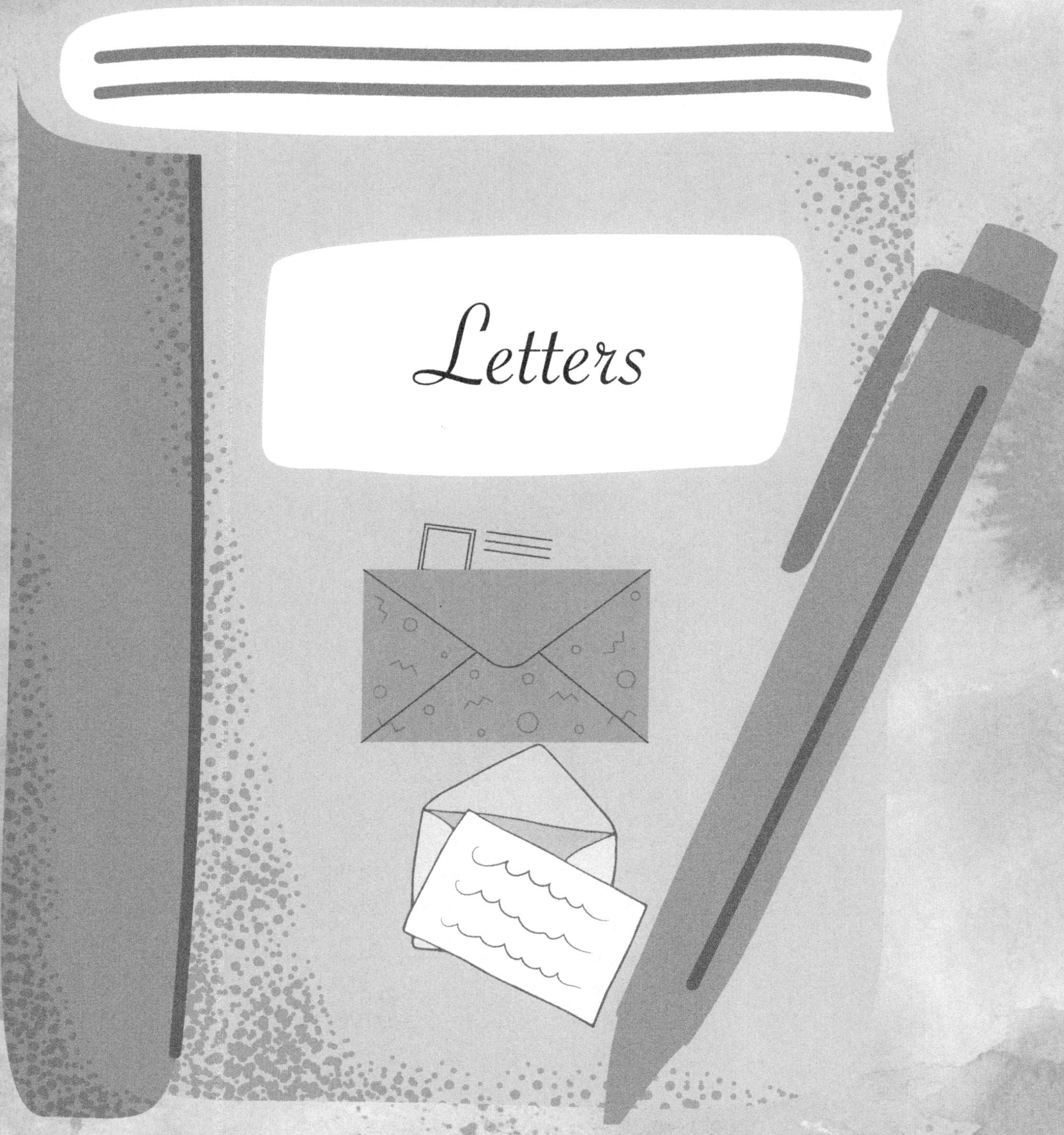

Letters

Write a letter to tell them how much they mean to you.

Date: _____

Dearest _____,

_____

_____

_____

_____

_____

_____

_____

_____

_____

_____

_____

_____

_____

Love,

_____

Letters

Write a letter to your loved one to tell them some exciting news.

Date: _____

Dearest _____,

Love,

_____

Letters

Write a letter to your loved one to tell them how you are doing now.

Date: _____

Dearest _____,

_____

_____

_____

_____

_____

_____

(

)

_____

_____

_____

_____

_____

_____

_____

_____

Love,

_____

Letters

Write a letter to your loved one to tell them about your struggles and challenges since they've been gone.

Date: _____

Dearest _____,

_____

_____

_____

_____

_____

_____

_____

_____

_____

_____

_____

_____

_____

Love,

_____

Letters

Write a letter to your loved one to tell them you're going to be okay.

Date: _____

Dearest _____,

_____

_____

_____

_____

_____

_____

_____

_____

_____

_____

_____

_____

Love,

_____

Letters

What do you wish you could apologize for but didn't get a chance to? What do you want to tell them now? Write it in this letter.

Date: _____

Dearest _____,

_____
_____
_____
_____
_____
_____
_____
_____
_____
_____
_____
_____

Love,

_____

49

Letters

Is there anything that your loved one did that hurt you or caused you pain in the past? Can you forgive them? Write them a letter.

Date: _____

Dearest _____,

_____
_____
_____
_____
_____
_____
_____
_____
_____
_____
_____
_____
_____
_____
_____
_____
_____
_____
_____
_____

Love,

_____

Letters

Are there any relatives you need to contact and talk to about what happened to your loved one? Write a letter to tell them.

Date: _____

Dearest _____,

_____

_____

_____

_____

_____

_____

_____

_____

_____

_____

_____

_____

Love,

_____

Letters

Are you talking to your friends about what you are going through?
It may be hard to start the conversation. Write a letter to tell them.

Date: _____

Dearest _____,

_____

_____

_____

_____

_____

_____

_____

_____

_____

_____

_____

_____

_____

_____

Love,

_____

Letters

Date: _____

Dearest _____,

Love,

_____

It takes more bravery to show your emotions than to hide them . . . to grieve well is to be emotionally strong.

—Unknown

Feelings & Emotions

How do you feel?

Look at the feeling words below. Circle five feelings you have felt in the last month. Write about each of them in the boxes provided and explain why you felt that way—what experiences or events led to these feelings? You may add your own words if you'd like.

joyful

anxious

excited

happy

hopeful

sad

devastated
scared
exhausted
stressed
overwhelmed
shocked

disappointed
tired
grateful
worried
confused
frustrated

lonely

angry

ashamed

relieved

surprised

guilty

What does it mean to you?

Look at each of the words or phrases. What do they mean to you? How does it make you feel to see or hear these words? Write down your thoughts or any other words or phrases that come to mind.

living

dying

mourning

grief/to grieve

losing a loved one

Mixed Emotions

You may be feeling many different emotions during this time. It's perfectly normal. Don't feel bad or guilty about the way you feel. All of your emotions are valid.

Think about a special memory you have of your loved one. How does it make you feel? If this emotion was a color, what would it be? What other emotion(s) come to mind? What color would that be? If you mix these colors together, what new color will you create? The emotions—like the colors—do not cancel each other out, they create something new.

Create something:
Get some different color paints, and squirt some out into a mixing bowl. Slowly mix them together as you think about your special memory and how you are feeling. Use the paint to write your emotions on the paper. Draw or paint a picture of your special memory. Make some patterns on the paper.

Mixed Emotions

Variations:

• Put a blob of the different color paints you have chosen on a piece of paper. Fold the paper in half so that the different color paints mix together and form a pattern on the paper.

• Make different color sand or salt using chalk or coloring powder, and pour them into a clear bottle. Look at how the sand or salt mix together.

• Use ink or food coloring to drop into a bowl of water. Use a toothpick or stick to slowly mix the ink or make a pattern in the water. Place a piece of paper on the water and lift it gently to see the lovely pattern it creates. You can also try tie-dyeing with a rolled up sock, shirt, cloth, etc.

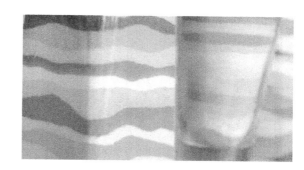

Mixed Emotions

Take a photo of your 'Mixed Emotions' masterpiece and stick it on this page. Give it a title and write a few sentences to describe it.

_____

_____

_____

_____

Design a Photo Frame

Buy a plain photo frame and personalize it with your own design. Paint over it, add sequins, glitter, or stickers. On a piece of paper or card, write statements and descriptions of what your loved one was like and how they have impacted your life or made you feel. Use different color pens, decorate and personalize it with drawings and pictures, add their photo, stickers or stamps etc. Insert it into the photo frame. See the example below.

DADDY

You were always so <u>patient</u>, even when I asked you the same questions over and over again, you still answered and helped me every single time.

Your words were full of <u>wisdom</u>. You have taught me so much about life and how to live with purpose and humility.

You have always been my <u>cheerleader</u>, and supported every dream I ever had. You even believed in me when I didn't believe in myself.

You were so <u>faithful</u>. Though your body grew weaker and weaker, your faith never did. I am a Christ follower today because of you.

Grief, I've learned, is really just love. It's all the love you want to give, but cannot. . . Grief is just love with no place to go.

— Jamie Anderson

Favorite Things

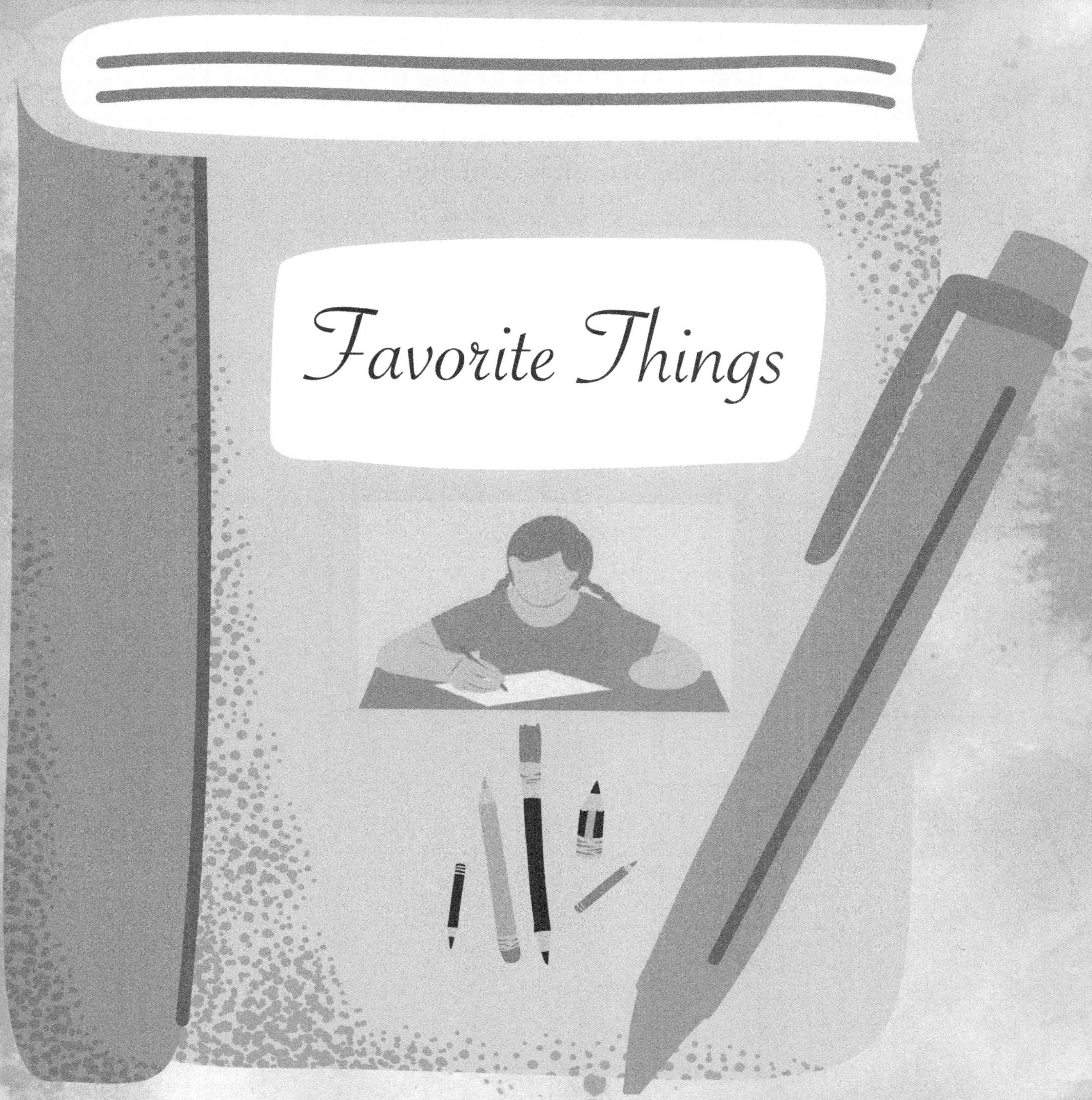

Favorite Place

What was your loved one's favorite place? What is it like? What can you see or do there? Why did they like it? How do you feel when you go there now? Write a description of the place. Take a photo the next time you go there, or draw a picture of it.

Date: _____

_____

_____

_____

_____

_____

_____

_____

_____

_____

_____

_____

Favorite Dishes

What were some of your loved one's favorite dishes? Were there any special recipes they used?

- Make a list of their favorite dishes.
- Make some of the dishes and write down the recipes.
- Draw a picture of the dishes or take a photo.
- Enjoy the dishes with your friends and family and share some happy memories together.
- Write about what the experience was like.

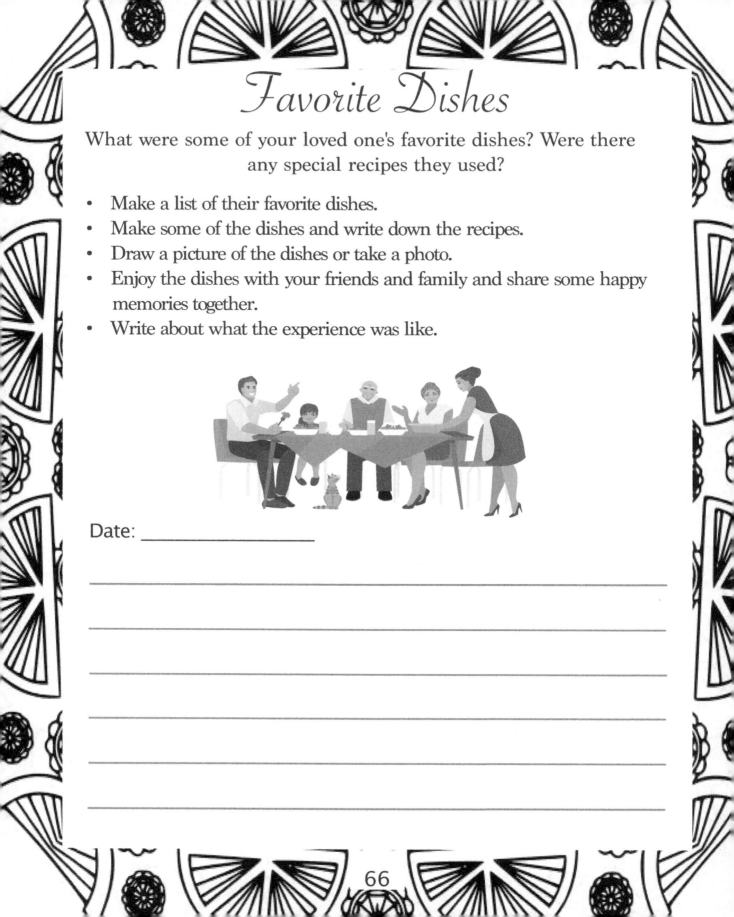

Date: _____

_____

_____

_____

_____

_____

Recipe

Favorite Songs

Make a playlist of your loved one's favorite songs.

Date: _____

Playlist

Song Title	Artist

Favorite Songs

Choose a song from the playlist. Listen and meditate on the song. Close your eyes and pay attention to the thoughts and feelings that come into your mind. Write them down.

Date: _____

Song Title: _____ Artist: _____

Favorite Songs

Rewrite the lyrics to one of the songs, or write your own version.

Date: _____

Favorite Songs

Draw a picture while you listen to your loved one's favorite song.

Date: _____

Favorite Movies

What were your loved one's favorite movies or TV shows? Why did they like it? What were some of their favorite parts of the movie or show? Which character did they most relate to and why? How do you feel when you watch it now?

Date: _____

Favorite Books

What were some of your loved one's favorite books? Why did they like it? What is it about? What are some special or meaningful quotes from it? How do you feel when you read it now?

Date: _____

Healing does not come after grief, but rather through it. And you do not grieve by training yourself to stop missing your loved one; rather, by acknowledging how much you really do miss them.

—Unknown

Journal Prompts

Altered Book Journal

Sometimes, it can be difficult to express yourself in words. You may be inspired by a passage in a book instead. Use an old book to try creating your altered book journal. If you do not want to use a real book, you can photocopy a page from one of your favorite books instead, and try altering the text on the page and creating your own piece. Draw on the page, circle or highlight words that jump out at you. You can even stick some pictures on top of it.

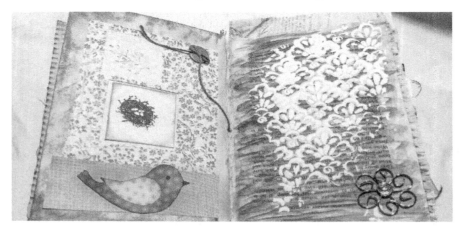

Look up these websites for more ideas and examples of Altered Book Journals:
https://artjournalist.com/how-to-prepare-an-old-book/
https://www.midmodernmama.com/altered-book-journal/

Journal

SOMETHING NEW

Write about a new experience. Maybe you have learned something,
made a friend or started a hobby?

Date: _____

_____

_____

_____

_____

_____

_____

_____

_____

_____

Journal

CHANGE OF PERSPECTIVE

Write about something that you have learned during this process and how it has changed the way you view your life and experiences.

Date: _____

_____

_____

_____

_____

_____

_____

_____

_____

_____

Journal

SHARING MY GRIEF

Have you been able to share openly about your grief with someone? Who did you talk to? How did you feel afterwards? If you haven't shared yet, who would want to talk to and what would you like to say?

Date: _____

_____

_____

_____

_____

_____

_____

_____

_____

_____

Journal

CHANGES

What are some changes you've experienced since you lost your loved one?

Date: _____

_____

_____

_____

_____

_____

_____

_____

_____

_____

_____

Journal

REGRET

Is there anything that you regret about the past? Maybe it's something you said or did; or didn't say or do.

Date: _____

_____

_____

_____

_____

_____

_____

_____

_____

_____

_____

_____

_____

WHAT I AM THINKING

Take a moment to listen to your thoughts. What are you thinking?
How are you feeling? Write down everything that comes to your
mind, like a stream of consciousness.

Date: _____

_____

_____

_____

_____

_____

_____

_____

_____

_____

_____

Journal

PRAYER

Write a prayer to ask God or your higher power for help in your grieving journey, thank Him for what He's done for you, or simply share your feelings and sorrow. Write down some helpful Scriptures.

Date: _____

_____

_____

_____

_____

_____

_____

_____

_____

_____

_____

There are no good-byes for us. Wherever you are, you will always be in my heart.

— Ghandi

Free Journaling

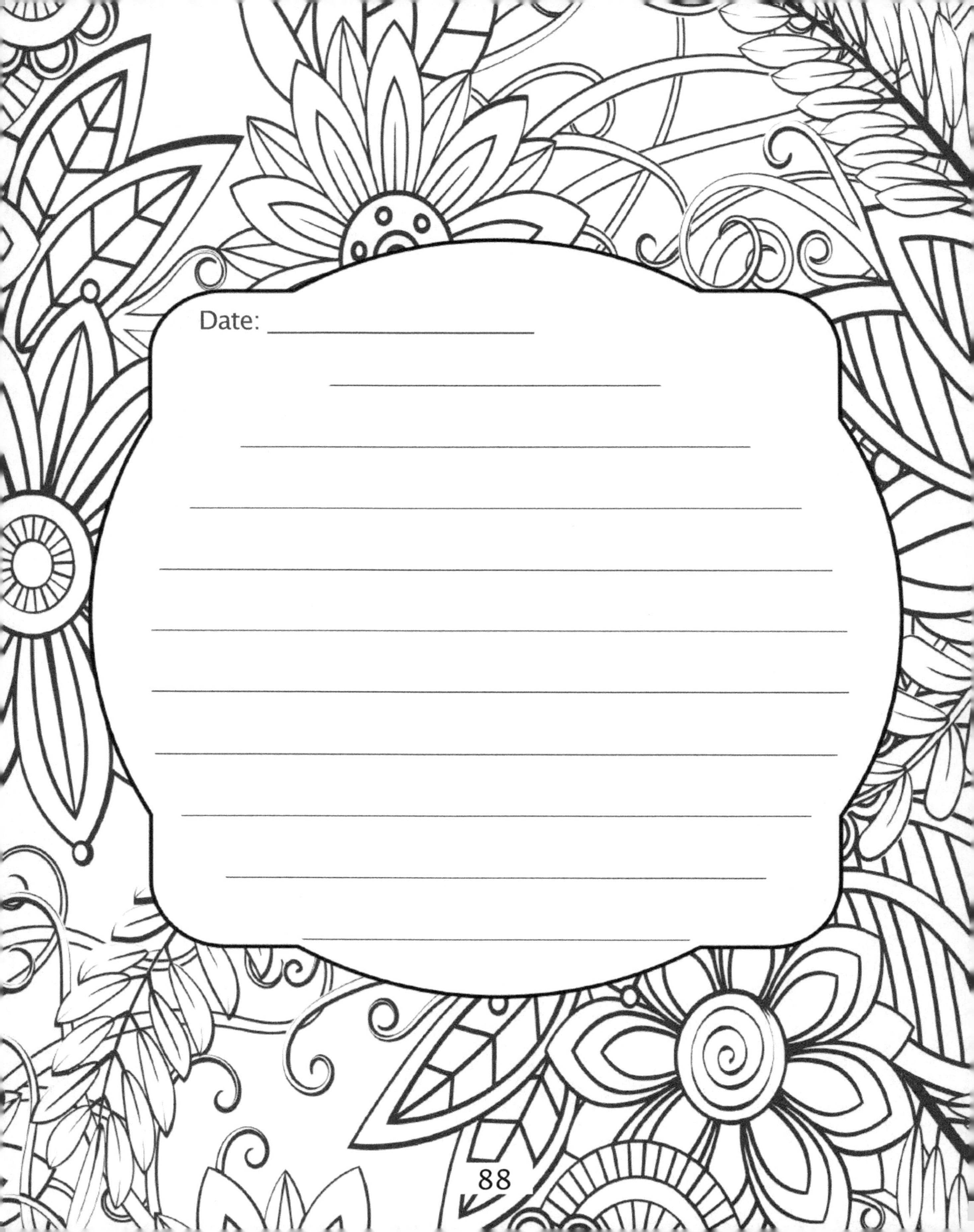

Date: _____

_____

_____

_____

_____

_____

_____

_____

_____

_____

Date: _____

Date: _____

_____

_____

_____

_____

_____

Date: _____

_____

_____

_____

_____

_____

Date: _____

Date: _____

Date: _____

Date: _____

_____

_____

_____

_____

_____

_____

_____

_____

_____

_____

_____

Date: _____

Wherever a beautiful soul has been there is a trail of beautiful memories.

— Ronald Reagan

Drawing & Coloring

Draw

Draw a picture of your favorite memory.

Date: _____

Draw

Draw a picture related to a prompt in the previous sections.

Date: _____

Draw

Draw a picture of your loved one doing their favorite activity.

Date: _____

Draw

Date: _____

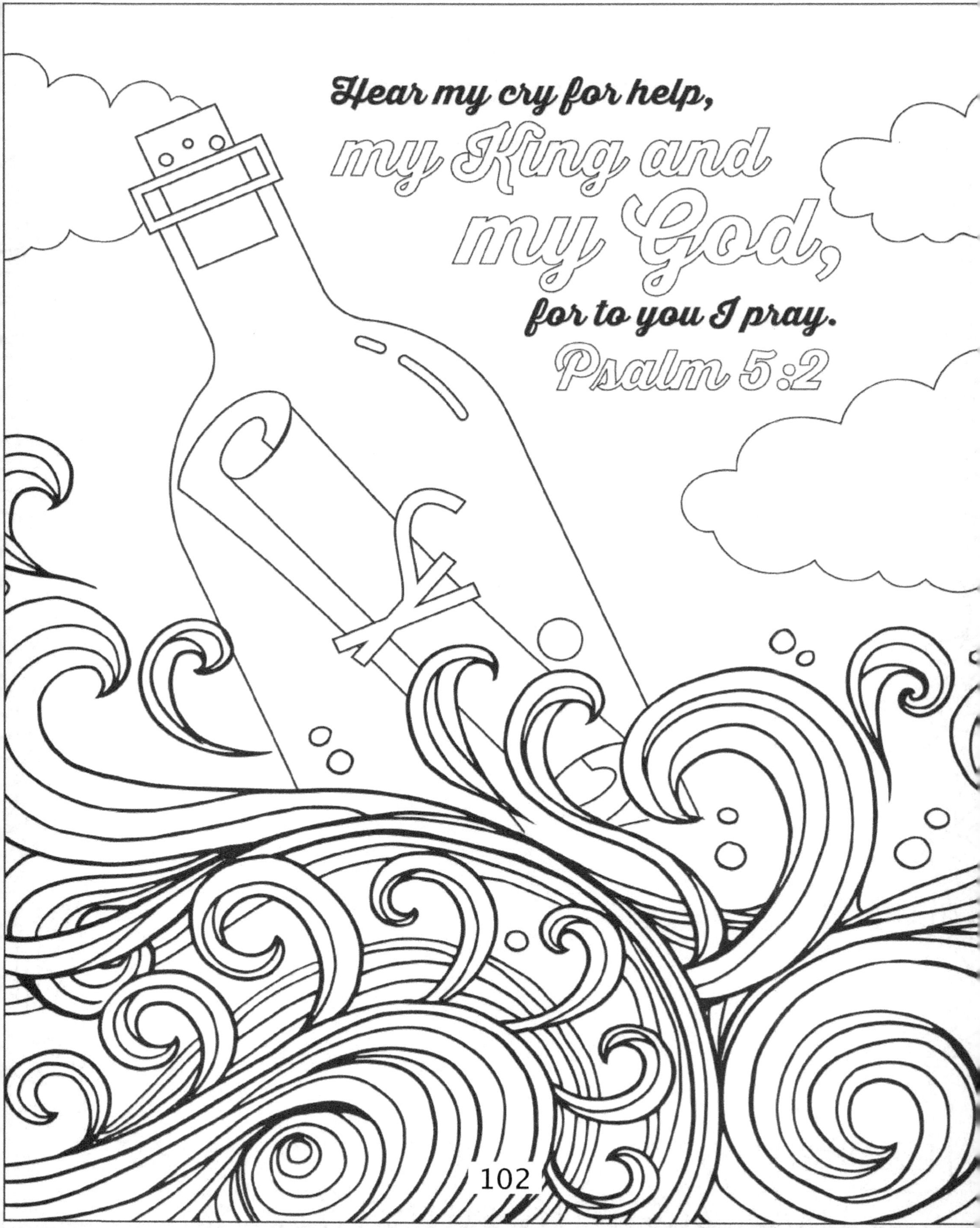
Hear my cry for help,
my King and
my God,
for to you I pray.
Psalm 5:2

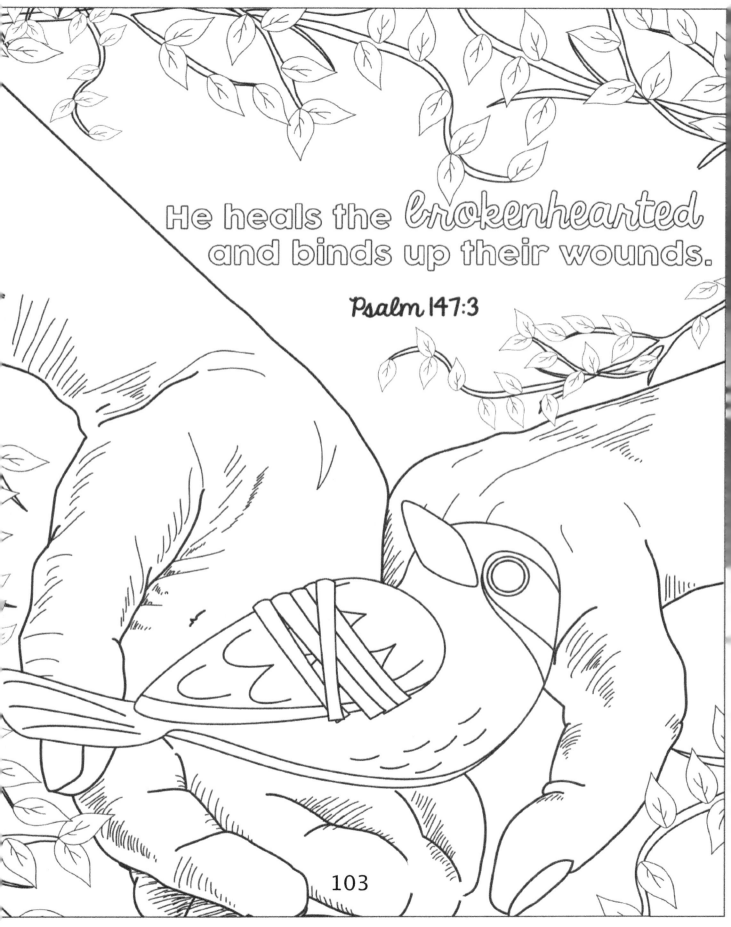

He heals the *brokenhearted* and binds up their wounds.

Psalm 147:3

103

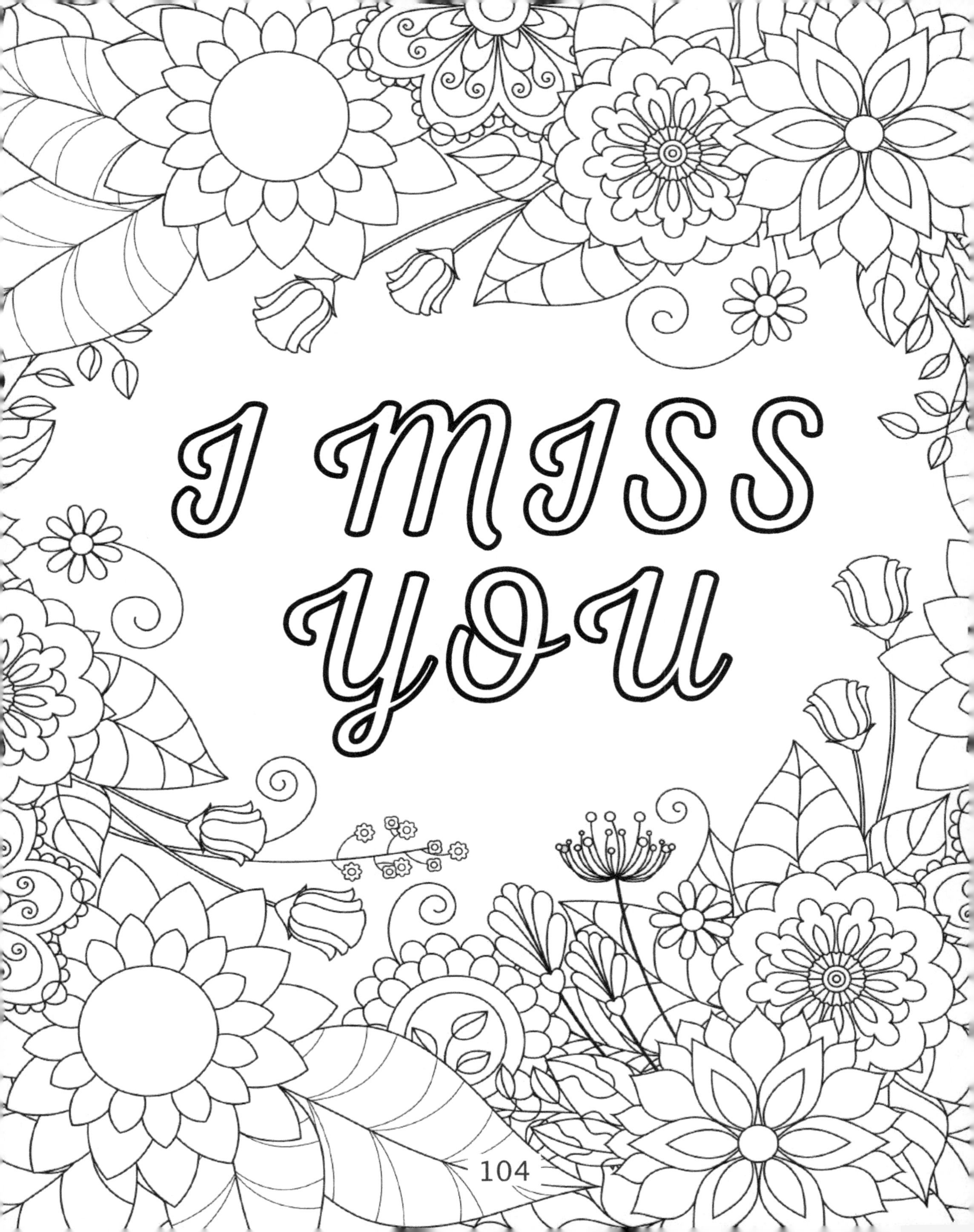
I MISS
YOU

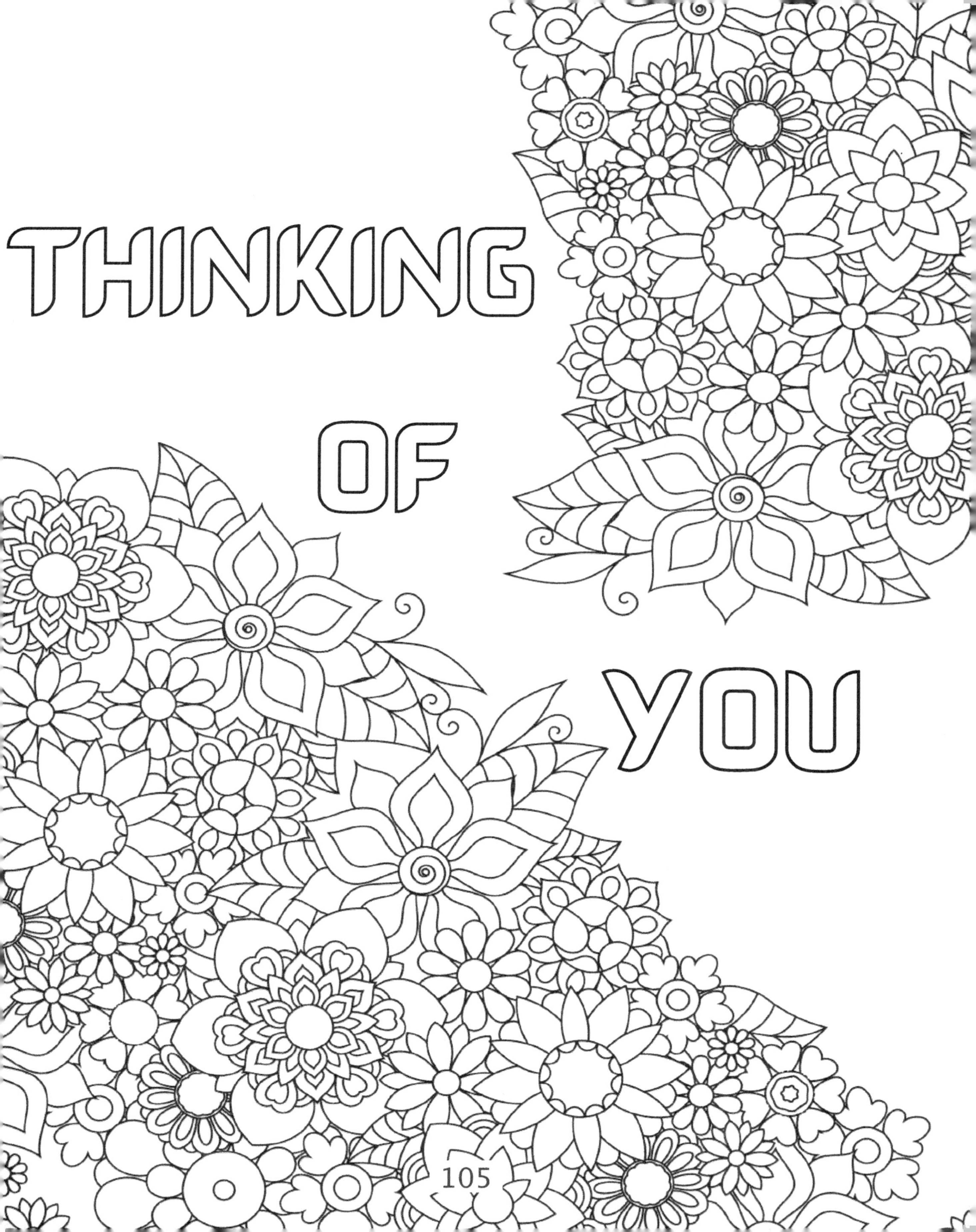
THINKING
OF
YOU

FOREVER IN MY HEART

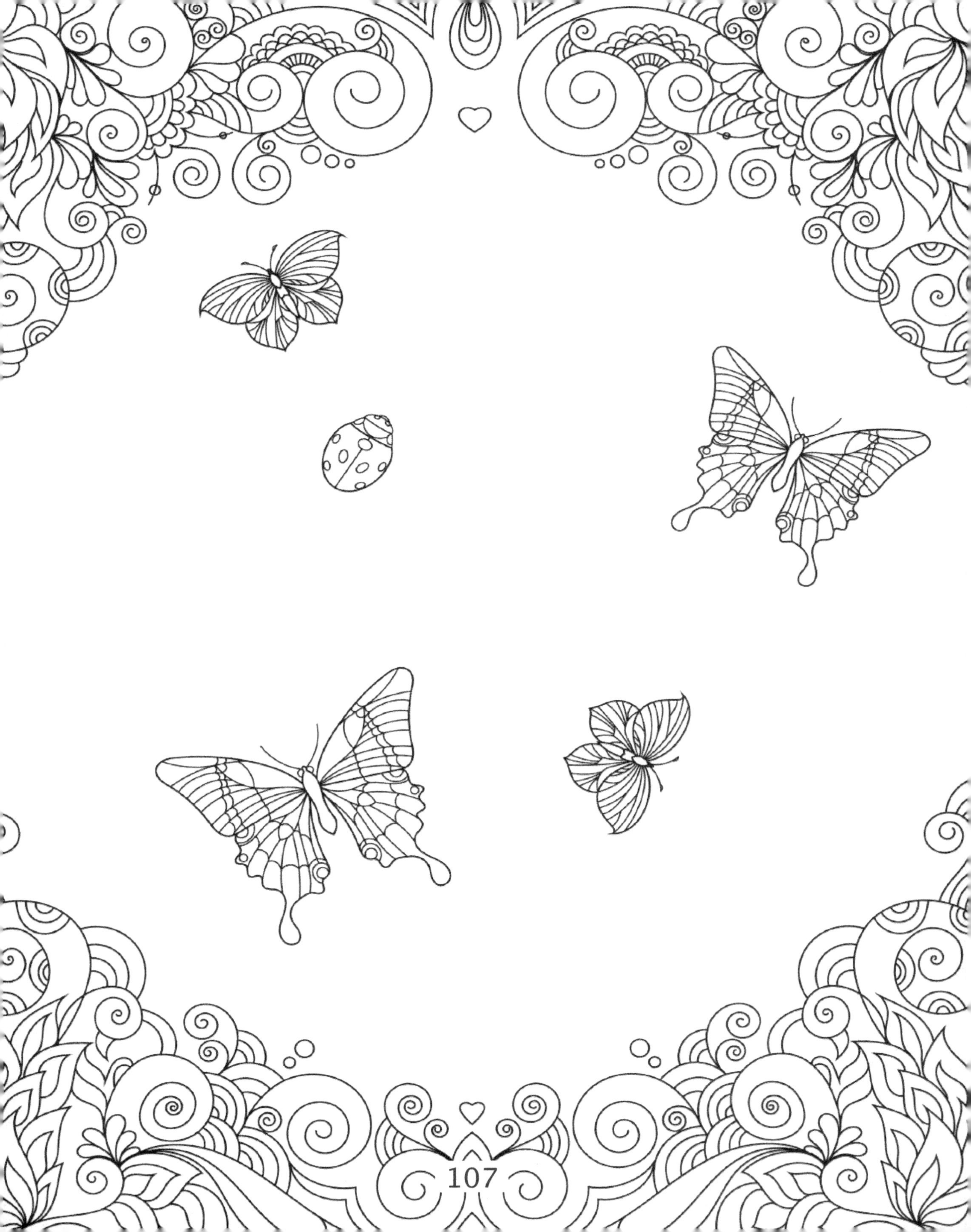

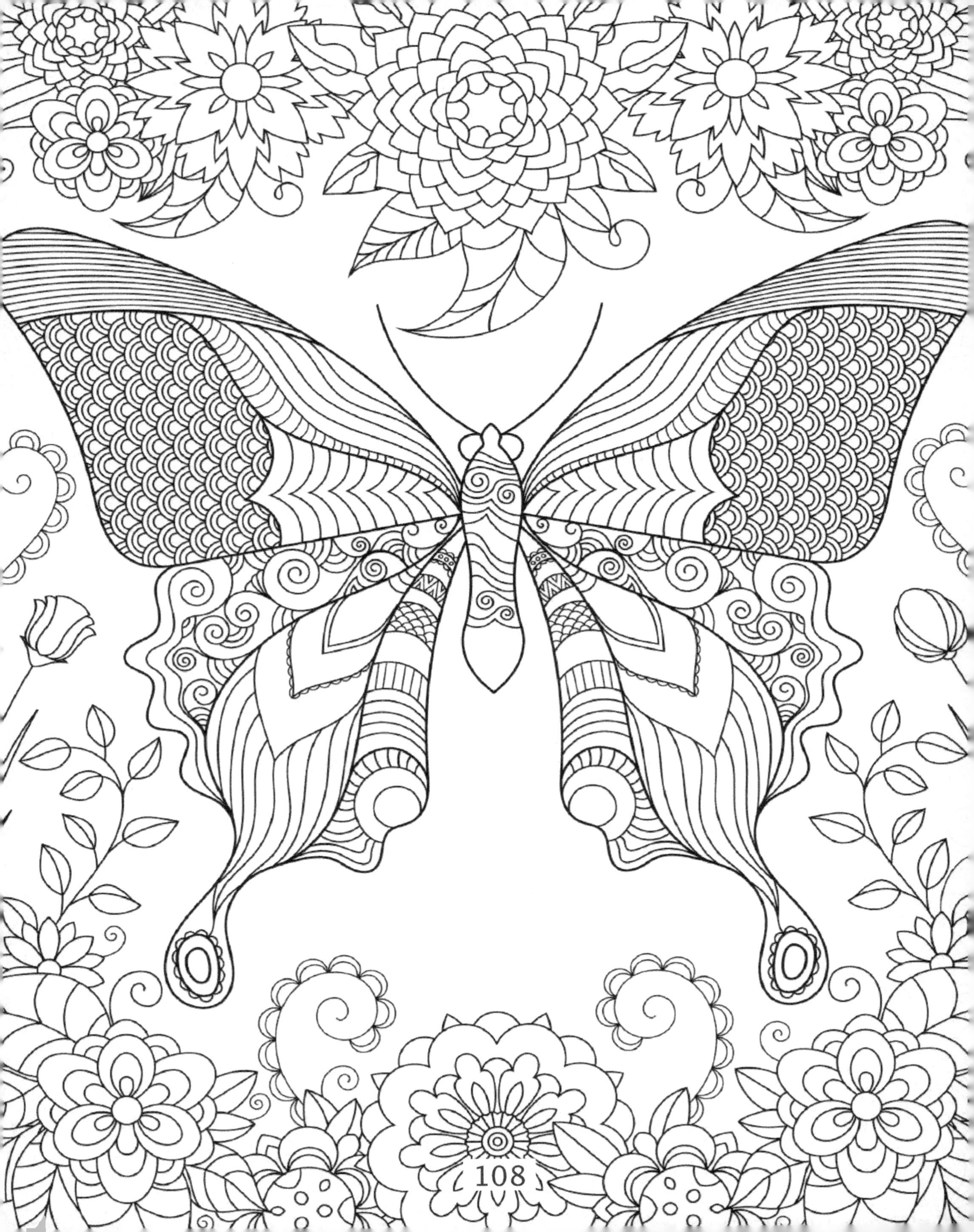

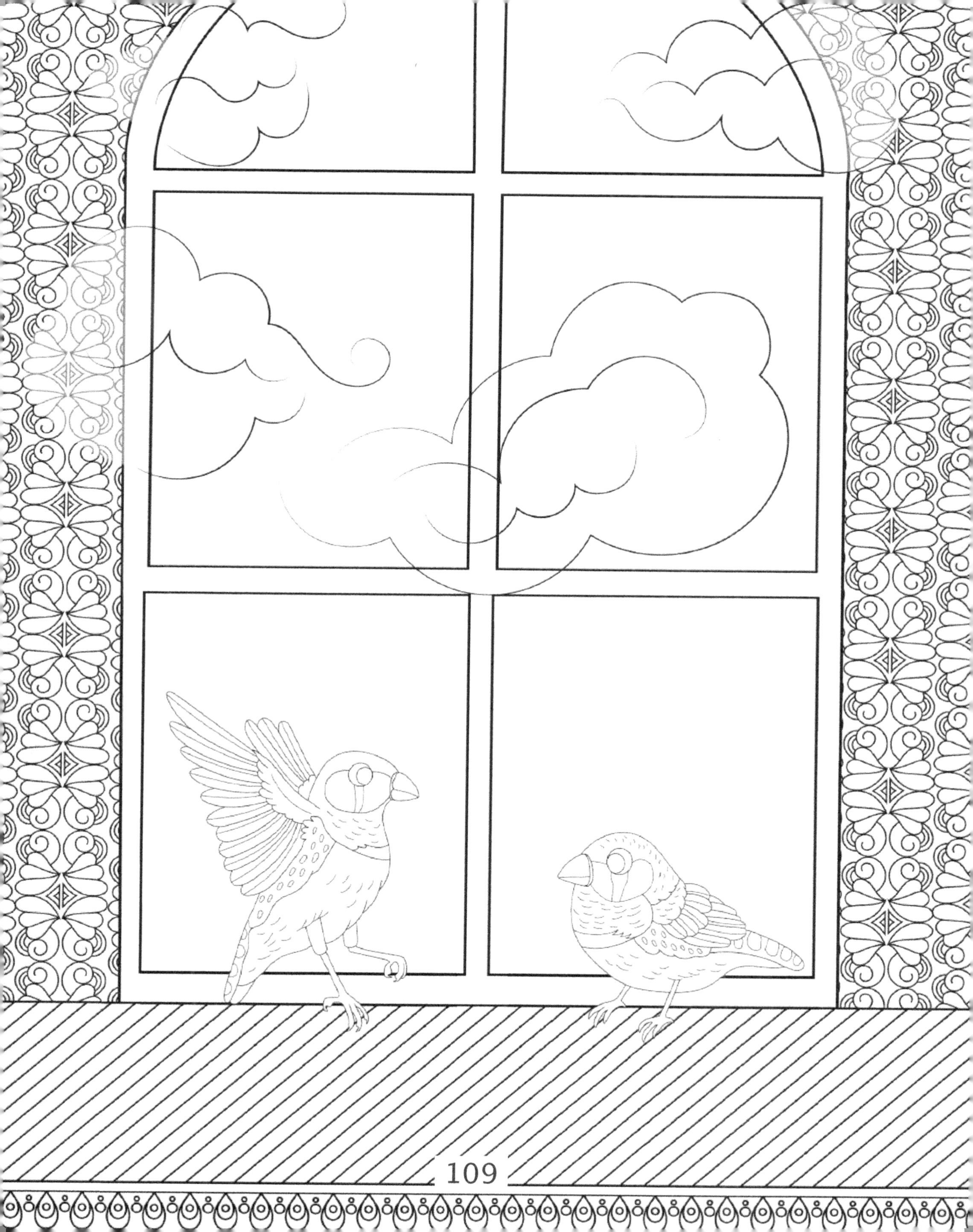

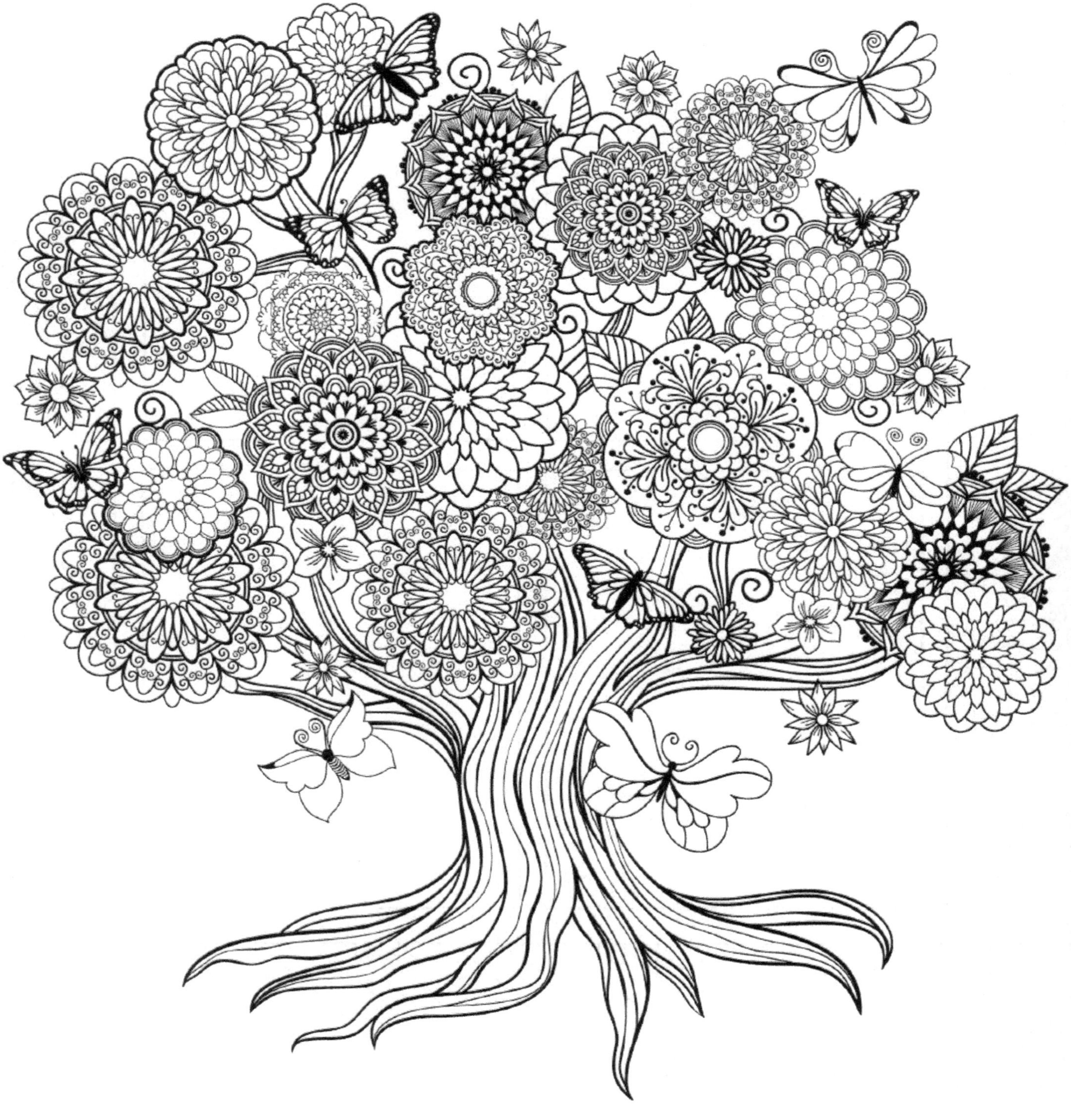

Grief never ends, but it changes. It's a passage, not a place to stay. Grief is not a sign or weakness, nor a lack of faith. It is the price of love.

–Unknown

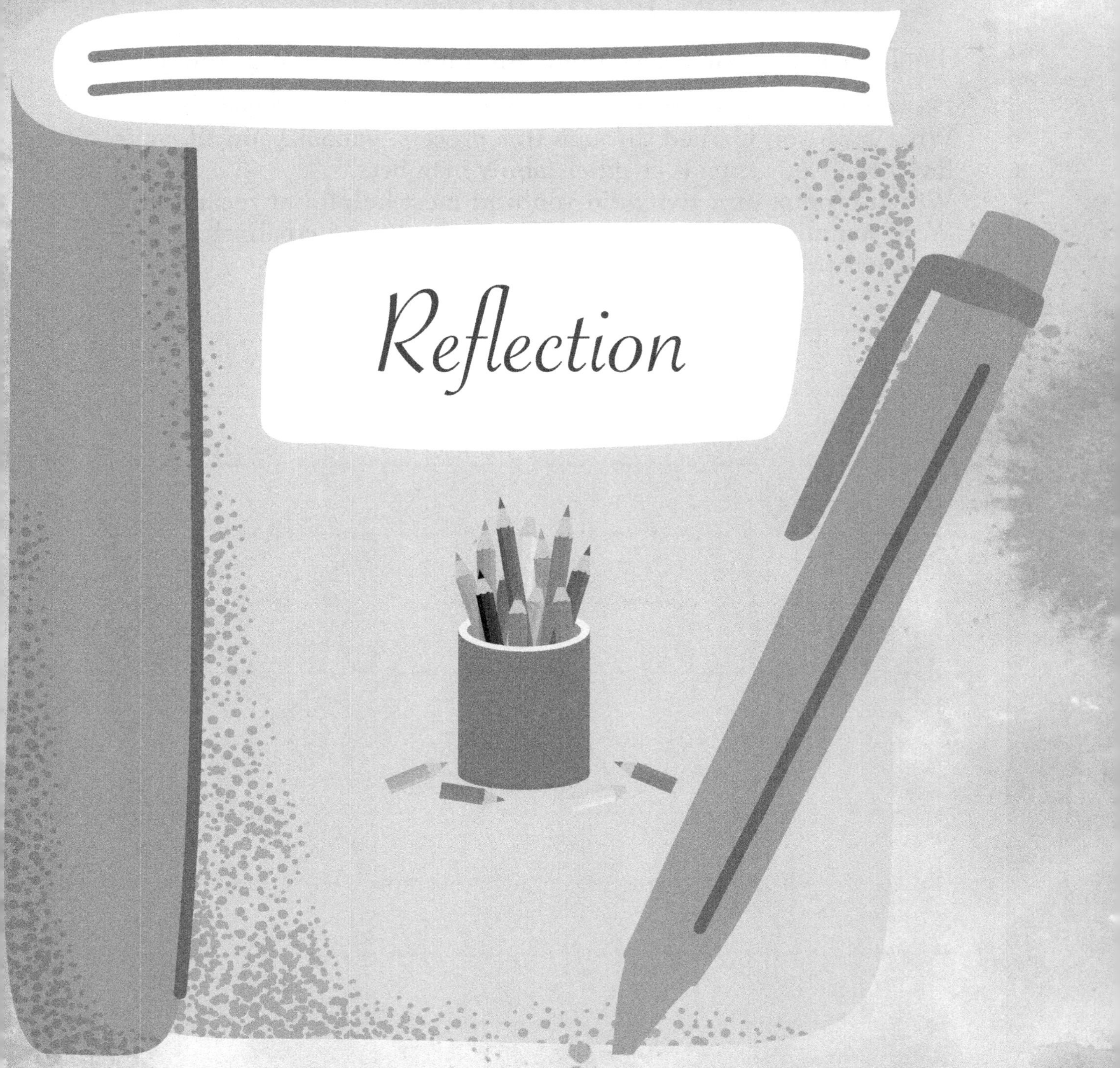
Reflection

Reflection

Look back at what you've done and take some time to reflect.

- Do you notice any changes in your feelings, moods, perspectives?
- What have you learned through this process – about yourself, your loved one, your friends or other family members?
- Which prompt or activity did you find most helpful or meaningful?
- Were you able to express yourself more freely and creatively?
- How has this helped you in your grieving process?

Date: _____

_____

_____

_____

_____

_____

_____

_____

_____

The reality is that you will grieve forever. You will not get over the loss of a loved one; you will learn to live with it. You will heal and you will rebuild yourself around the loss you have suffered. You will be whole again but you will never be the same. Nor should you be the same nor would you want to.

– Elisabeth Kübler-Ross

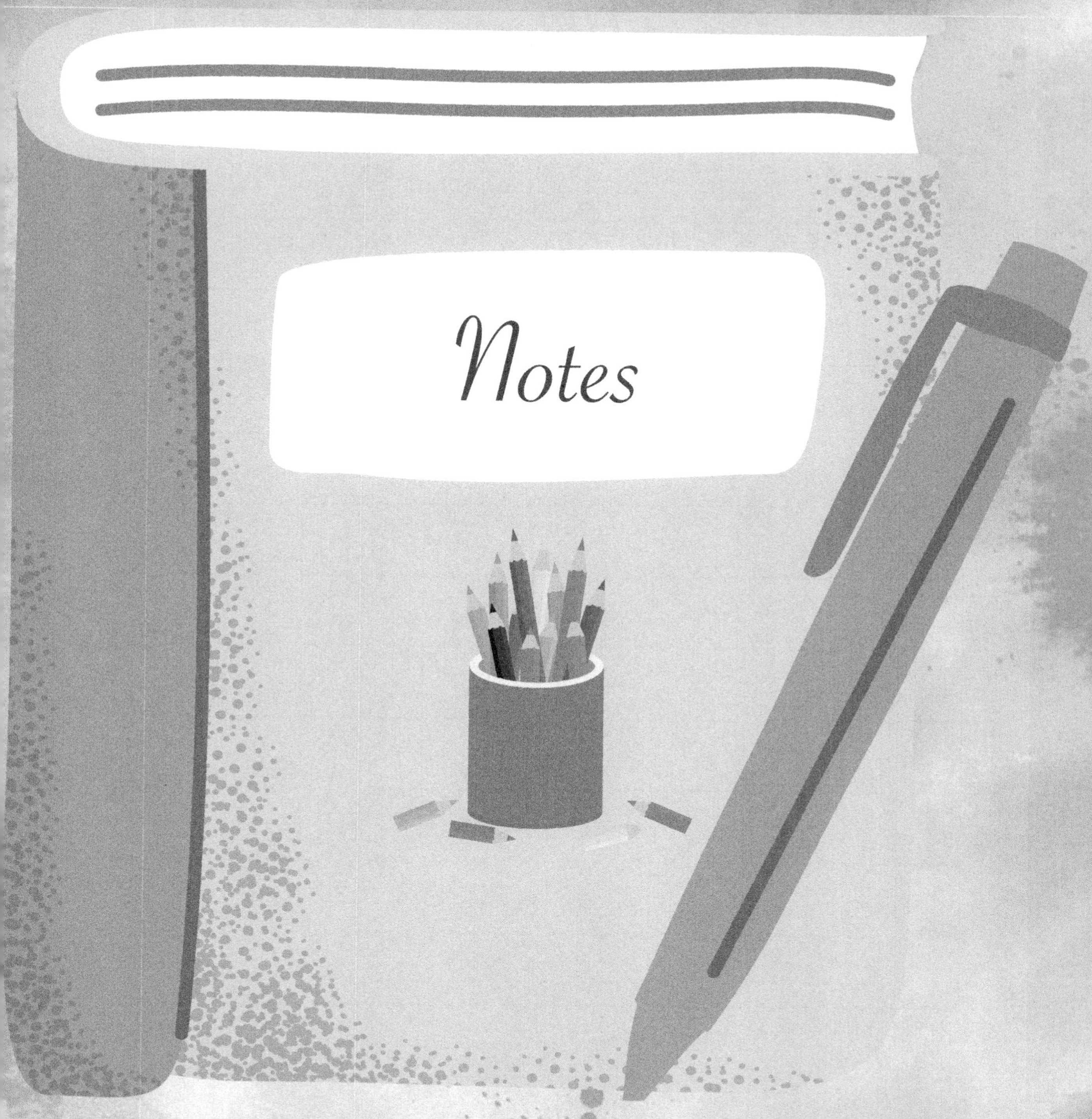
Notes

Notes

Notes

Notes

Notes

Dedications

This journal is dedicated to all our loved ones in Heaven–taken from us too soon, but will forever live on in our hearts.

~

Just weeks before publishing this journal, one of the most supportive and kindest authors in the children's book community passed away. He will be dearly missed by all who knew him. This is a special dedication to him...

To James Roberts, AKA Gentleman Jim (1966-2022),
You've been an amazing friend and supportive member of #authorforce. Even though we have only known each other for a few years, you are still hands-down one of the kindest people I have ever known. You have made this author journey a joy. Thank you for all your support and encouragement. I will miss your smile, silly jokes, children's books and reviews, bow ties, Velocikitty, and your big big heart! May you rest in peace, my friend.
Keep dapper! Authors Assemble!

Y.Y.

Acknowledgements

This journey has not been easy and I couldn't have done it without the kindness and support of so many wonderful people in the author and writing community. Every time I felt like giving up, you all lifted me up with your sweet words of encouragement and endless support. I'm so grateful for everyone in our #authorforce community and everyone who has provided their feedback and suggestions during the production of this journal. Thank you to those who have volunteered their time and effort to support the launch and helped to share about this journal. I appreciate it so much!

Thank you to my mom, who has encouraged me to keep chasing my dreams and doing what I love. Thank you to my dad, grandmas and grandpas who are all in Heaven. You have all left a legacy that will live on forever in my heart, and have inspired me to create this journal to help others on the lifelong journey of grief. I miss you all so much but I know that I can still talk to you whenever and wherever I want because you have never left my heart.

Thank you to my Heavenly Father, who continues to lead and light the way, guiding me to where I need to go. You have answered all my prayers and prepared this amazing plan for my life, beyond my wildest dreams. I have finally found my purpose in life.

About the Author

Y. Y. Chan was born in Hong Kong but grew up in sunny Brisbane, Australia where she had Christmas during summer. She returned to Hong Kong to teach English after graduating from university with First Class Honours. She also has an M.A. in English Language Teaching, and has been teaching English for over ten years.

When her father passed away, she took a break from teaching to travel, read, and write. She now teaches English and works freelance for different educational institutes.

Can You Hear Me, Daddy? is her debut picture book, and winner of the Royal Dragonfly Book Award. When she is not writing or teaching, she is either reading or looking for more books to add to her overflowing bookshelf.

To see news and updates on her work, go to https://www.yychani.com to subscribe.
Follow on Social Media:
Facebook: https://www.facebook.com/yychanauthor
Instagram: https://www.instagram.com/yychan_author
Twitter: https://www.twitter.com/yychan_author

Other Books By Y. Y. Chan

Can You Hear Me, Daddy?

It's not easy to talk to your kids about death and grief. With this book, readers can be uplifted and learn about how faith in Christ can bring us peace and comfort. This book aims to help families, schools and communities start conversations about death, loss and grief.
(Royal Dragonfly Book Award 1st & 2nd Place Winner)
https://bit.ly/yychan-cyhmd

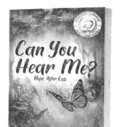

Can You Hear Me?: Hope After Loss

Can good things really come from bad things? Why does God allow bad things to happen? Will Daddy still be able to hear me from Heaven?
These are just some of the questions Renee starts thinking about after she finds out that her daddy has cancer. She documents all the things that are happening in her diary as she watches her daddy go through the stages of cancer. (Readers' Favorite Gold Medal Winner)
https://bit.ly/yychan-cyhm

My Reading Journal: A Guided Journal for Kids to Keep Track of Their Reading

This is the ultimate guided journal for kids aged 9+. It is packed with reading tips and strategies, together with a wide range of reflection tasks and questions to help kids dig deeper into what they are reading, and find meaning and relevance to their own lives.
https://bit.ly/yychan-MRJ

Grandma, It's Me!: A Children's Book about Dementia

This uplifting and touching story encourages young readers to support and care for the elderly with love, patience and understanding. Grandma, It's Me! also encourages journaling as a way to process emotions and feelings in order to become resilient to face life's many challenges. It has received five-star reviews from Readers' Favorite, and has been recommended by dementia caregivers and professionals.
https://bit.ly/yychan-grandma

Can You Help?

I hope that this journal has helped you through this challenging process of grief and you have found some ways to express your feelings and emotions through the prompts provided in this journal. It would mean so much to me if you could spare a few minutes to leave an honest review on whichever platform or retailer you have purchased this journal, and share about how it has helped you. This helps to get the journal noticed by more people who may be interested and need a journal like this.

Thank you so much for your support!

Made in the USA
Middletown, DE
08 May 2023

30239060R00073